Ghost Town Street

By the Same Author

The Honicknowle Book of the Dead
A Long Weekend on the Sofa
Love Letter to an Imaginary Girlfriend

Kenny Knight

Ghost Town Street

Shearsman Books

First published in the United Kingdom in 2025 by
Shearsman Books Ltd
PO Box 4239
Swindon
SN3 9FN

Shearsman Books Ltd Registered Office
30–31 St. James Place, Mangotsfield, Bristol BS16 9JB
(this address not for correspondence)

EU AUTHORISED REPRESENTATIVE:
Lightning Source France, 1 Av. Johannes Gutenberg, 78310 Maurepas, France
Email: compliance@lightningsource.fr

www.shearsman.com

ISBN 978-1-83738-009-1

Copyright © Kenny Knight, 2025
The right of Kenny Knight to be identified as the author
of this work has been asserted by him in accordance with the
Copyrights, Designs and Patents Act of 1988.
All rights reserved.

ACKNOWLEDGEMENTS
Some of the poems in this collection have previously been published in
International Times, *Lay of the Land*, *Litter*, *Shearsman* magazine, *Stride*,
Tears in the Fence.

Many thanks to Sara Elizabeth Smiles and Steve Spence
for all their assistance.

Contents

Friary House	9
Meetings in April	13
Missing You	14
George and the Goldfish	15
Thirteen Stars	17
The Hands of the Rich and the Hands of the Poor	19
On the Doorstep of the Grand Hotel	21
Ghost Town Street	23
Vikings	25
As If You Were	26
If a Vaccine Can't Be Found	28
Meeting Miss World	30
Blind Mouse	32
The Rook	33
The Poetry of Leonard Cohen	37
Knives, Forks and Coffee Spoons	40
Waiting for News	41
Discovering Little America	42
Getting Dressed in the Dark	44
Sixty-Nine	45
Take the Hand of Nancy Astor	47
Slowly Going Crazy	50
The Other Side of the Rain Puddle	51
Dropping Down in the West	53
Belper	54
The Last Year	56
Playing the Blues on Apsley Road	58
Gone to Make Coffee	60
Shopping on the Table	62
Pinball Lane	63
The Millionaire	65
Six Days after the Jab	67
Over the Rim of a Blue Bandana	69
Down and Out on Downshire Hill	75

The Radio Years	77
Elm Road	78
Rufus	79
Hartley Park	84
Ursula	86
The Narrow Road to the Deep West	93
The Long Lost Shadows of Saturday Night	94
The Ghost Writers Club	95
Reading Baudelaire in April	97
Ghost Town Year	99
Looking for Yellow	101
Waiting for William	103
Gosport	105
Goodbye Ghost Town Street	106
Glossary	108

Ghost Town Street

for
Thom Boulton, Dan Hartigan & William Telford

Friary House

1

The day before the letter arrives
I go out walking
keeping a distance
a metre or two from my shadow
which moves ahead
but never far enough
to detach itself and be free.
I think of calling it back
like one would call to a dog
or throwing a stick to see if it runs.
I wave and it waves back.

2

On the eve of moving into exile
I discover a dozen benches
along the Atlantic seafront
where the dead sit with friends,
sometimes strangers.
I know this place
this feeling of loss.

I make a telescope
out of my writing hand
gaze through a tunnel of ink stains
see other shadows out walking
in groups or pairs
think about what breed of dog
I'd like my shadow to be
one that doesn't bark too much
one that doesn't walk by itself.
Only silence and rainfall

I conclude will come between us.
Crossing Madeira Road I turn for home
leaving the sunshine and the world
of coughs and sneezes behind
and unknown to me at this point,
surrendering my freedom
on the doorstep of number ten.

3

On the day the letter arrives
telling me not to leave my home
for eighty-four days
I take George Orwell
down from the bookshelf
and we go walking
through the kitchen together
like two down and outs
with nowhere else to go.
The writer and the ghostwriter.
Bretonside and Paris.
Freedom Fields and Catalonia.

Restless for the chatter of the crowd
we skate across the 20/20 darkness
but nothing moves
out on the streets of the town.
The city is as empty as a seashell.

If it were safe
for George and I to leave here
we'd go walking together
along Ghost Town Street
feeding hungry flocks of seagulls
strutting for the surveillance cameras
like extras in an Alfred Hitchcock remake.

All that's needed now
is to slip into a reindeer jumper
pop a bottle of champagne
and glug glug glug
we could play Santa Claus.
Unwrapping freedom
we could send a Christmas card
to Patrick McGoohan in Portmeirion
make make-believe rocket noises
or fake a landing on the rooftop
instead of hanging around here
for eighty-four days
listening to The Groundhogs.

4

After playing to the absent crowd
I return to the kitchen
drop a pyramid into hot water
blink and a sequence of mirages occur.
Camels on the cobbled back lane.
Parking meters turning into Daleks
chasing drivers back to their cars.
A golden palace pulled like a cardigan
over the head of the barcode.
Pyramid in hand I blink again
head for the oasis of the sofa
thoughtfully plonk myself down
to read undercover, paperback in hand.

5

After reading a little bit of George
I take a telephone call from his older brother
who calls fleetingly before vanishing

like the last of the summer winos
into the vaults of the underground.
George's brother is a man of secrets
a man of mystery, a man of red tape,
another classified pedestrian
on Threadneedle Street,
a Cambridge graduate on a West End escalator
the first in line to the family's portfolio
hidden underneath a Swiss Cottage mattress.
I imagine him travelling on the Northern Line
between Camden Town and Belsize Park.
I think of him now in that tin of sardines
another newspaper reader in a pin-striped mask
hanging off a two-hundred-year-old broadsheet line
heading for the chandelier at the end of the tunnel.
The train passes under the Roundhouse
and the soundtracks of my bohemian youth.
Within the hour George's older brother
will be on the blower
will be looking back at Westminster
from the family home on Parliament Hill
the corridors where he walked with Florence
the little coffee shop on Berkeley Square.

Meetings in April

I meet the nightingale
out walking in April
on the corner of Dorothy Ward Lane.
We exchange greetings
in Japanese and English.
She points to a wildflower
the white and yellow head of a daisy
growing on this highway of footsteps
its slender neck sticking up through
a crack in the pavement.

I write her a haiku
with too many lines

too many stanzas
too many syllables.

I meet the waitress.
She feeds me bars of so much delight
and I meet the bubble car lady
I've seen her twice now
driving backwards through Speedwell City
taking one last look at the sea.

Missing You

I miss you and I miss the crowds
my social life has dwindled
to an island the size
of a four-letter word.

I miss your freckles
the seeds that bloom into promises
every time you smile.

I miss the traffic jams
the bumper-to-bumper intimacies.
I swing like a pendulum
between solitude, loss
and slipping into your arms.

I miss your company
and I miss your kindness.
You caught my eye
and threw it back.

The sun is out
and so is the rain.
I haven't cried so much
since the night you left.
I must have swallowed a cloud
or a broken heart.

Every day I go out walking
but you're not there.

I take your photograph
out of my memory
pin it up all over the sky
look for you amongst the masks.

George and the Goldfish

After another landline conversation tails off
like birdsong in the back yard
I talk garbage to a tank of goldfish
that spend the day swimming under lockdown glass
two or three metres apart

but then I realise
there aren't any goldfish
there isn't a tank
then I wonder whether
I'm having a flashback
so I write a note to remind myself
to stop talking to things
that aren't there
like George
who isn't a goldfish
remind myself to concentrate
on important things
like making shopping lists
a Papermate pen
a copy of *The Guardian*
toilet rolls
pasta
a bottle of disinfectant
a night out at the White House
a couple of thousand shares in Dettol
a calendar
something for the goldfish,
some pork sausages for George.

In the meantime
humming in the moonlight
the stock market crashes
while the world plays pinball

out on Ghost Town Street
I sit here
in my father's old armchair
on Nightingale Gardens
watching the sun set
over the rim of a red bandana.

Thirteen Stars

You can't go travelling
can't go to where
you'd like to be
the last flights have gone.
You're standing in your imagination
on the roundabout to somewhere else
hitch-hiking at the end of April
down to the Thirteen Stars
where every key hanging off a hook
opens a door to a different part of the world
once guests have checked into the lobby
they move from room to room.
There's no borderlines here
no luggage checks for contraband
no trips across the sky.

In room thirteen you can send
a postcard from Massachusetts.

In room four hundred
you can go sailing on the Speedwell
hang out on the Mayflower Steps
be a pilgrim or a pothead.

Room number nine has bat-swing doors
sometimes you just have to go in shooting
once you step inside tell the bartender
that you're here to see the dentist
to walk the graveyard streets of Tombstone
to dance with the widows of gunslingers
in Arizona's silver dust.

In room nine hundred and ninety-nine
you can spend the night

driving around London in a fire engine
while thinking about smoking dope
next door in Marrakesh
or tripping in a bicycle shed across the corridor-
an eight-hour psychedelic holiday
somewhere in the Swiss Alps.

Take the lift or take the stairs
up to the rooftop terrace
to see the skyscrapers
the mountain ranges of the world.
Ski back down to sea level
go underground – explore the basement
meet the grandchildren of Jules Verne.
Behind the door of room number six
the architecture looks Italian
but the dragon's Welsh.
Spend the afternoon in Portmeirion
face pressed against the window
years after McGoohan left town
then spin the atlas
when night falls to see
where the Thirteen Stars takes you next –
skinny dipping in St. Tropez
calling room service in Mongolia
or setting off in a snowstorm
from North Road Station
crossing Central Park
getting lost in New York
trying to find Outland Road.

The Hands of the Rich
and the Hands of the Poor

Last night down here
on Ghost Town Street
a mile or so from Friary House
I heard the sound
of many hands clapping
out on the cobbled lane.
Moving towards the window
I leaned out over the kitchen sink
saw neighbours clapping in backyards
to a song I couldn't hear
then I heard a whisper on the grapevine
then my shadow quietly hummed
the nightingale's song in my ear
and we joined in with the applause.

Last night on cobbled lanes
and cul-de-sacs all over the country
the old and the young
were banging saucepan lids
with knives and forks and silver spoons
the hands of the rich
and the hands of the poor
clapping for the doctors and the nurses
clapping all the way back
to nineteen forty-eight
clapping on the doorsteps
of Tredegar and Ebbw Vale
clapping in Derriford and Freedom Fields
clapping for the man who for me
is the grandfather I never had
the grandfather who gave my mother
a place to sleep
a place to give birth to three children

two girls and a boy
one in March
one in November
one on Christmas Day.

On the Doorstep of the Grand Hotel

I walk through the long grass
skirting the skateboarders
and the cyclists
the dogs and the seagulls
chasing tennis balls
chasing breadcrumbs
swooping in a scrum down
of fur and feathers
barking in the air.

Moving in a semi-circle
I leave the long grass
leave the wild
for the cultivated lawn
crossing the tarmac
to where the four of you
sat looking out to sea
in the summer of sixty-seven
and we all climbed on board
or we didn't.

My father never liked your music
thought you only knew one word
yeah guess he only
listened to the chorus.
I look out over the sea
at the island named after a saint
named after a pirate
I now call it the invisible island
as it slips into the fog
like my father's generation.

The seagulls are still here
heckling for fish and chips

and the girls that screamed at your gigs
are now old-age pensioners.
Guess they only listened to your music
in the quiet of their rooms.

I imagine my teenage self
sitting here at fifteen
banging the hell out of Ringo's drums.
Here on the doorstep of the Grand Hotel
where you sat looking out at the Atlantic.
A long way from playing live in Hamburg
at the Star Club.

I look across the Esplanade
look down the hill
at the ghost town traffic
at distant dog walkers
on Madeira Road.
I look into the faces
of strangers
into the eyes
of Redfern's
rock and roll photo.
Two of you are gone now
like so many this year.

Ghost Town Street

The first week is over
sleep seems to have been
not much longer than a sigh.
I call friends
mourn for company
develop narratives
when I should be dreaming.

I wait for someone
from the cafe to call
keep thinking about
handing in my notice
at the supermarket
and applying for a job
as a Zen Monk.

I make notes in my diary
after calling old friends
to arrange to meet for coffee
sometime in the next couple of years.

Now that I can't
hang out with the crowd
or shake anyone's hand
I'm getting closer to the trees.
It's springtime now
but with the number
of leaves falling
it feels like autumn

In the newspaper
I read the obituaries of people
who've died this week –
the lady who survived

two World Wars and the Spanish Flu
the doctors and the nurses
and the care home workers
who died because of a shortage
of gowns and masks.

Eighty-four days
waiting for the sun
to rise out of this nightmare.

Trying not to touch my face
trying not to rub my naked eyes
trying to stay two parking meters
away from the shadows
of neighbours and friends
trying not to shake
the hands of the invisible man
and his wife.

Sleeping when I can
and when I can't
taking a tea break
in the middle of the night
while waiting for another letter
from Friary House to set me free.
Until then the doormat is my border.
No-one waits outside
should I wish to cross
and go walking with the blues
along Ghost Town Street
walking with only
my shadow for company
blind to my suntanned reflection;
a fleeting film star
on double-decker windows
passing through town.

Vikings

The Vikings came here
over a thousand years
before the skateboarders
reached the end of the Esplanade

they came in long ships
from Iceland and Norway
 Sweden and Denmark

over a thousand years
before film stars sailed across
my mum's television screen
in Chatsworth Gardens

before this weird silence
fell over the deckchairs
they came to this island
speaking the language of the sea.

As If You Were

I have no past
I come and go, mostly unnoticed.
Here in the park there's a path
that runs down to Wollaton Grove.
I drift along the edge of the long grass
bring shade to buttercups,
dandelions, wild clover.
This is one of the parks
I walked through in your childhood.
I have no history
no memory of dresses
hanging from washing lines
though you say
there's something beautiful
in the moving shapes
they make along the ground.
I do not see the white butterflies
parachuting caterpillars
onto your father's cabbages.
I have never had a conversation with you
or your brother who lives in the glass.
I do not bark though you follow
like a detective.

I have no narrative
no nationality
no archive.
Sixty-eight autumns have gone
yet I only appeared in Freedom Fields
on the night you were born.
If there were tears on my face
they were only a quiet echo of yours.
I have no voice but the one
you give to me in this poem.

I do not speak your language
or Kafka's or Kundera's.
I do not speak the language of old houses
like a mouse or a jackdaw.
I have been tripping with you
to Chalk Farm and Llandegley
but have never had a flashback
or a postcard
from one of your colourful friends.
You're an old-age pensioner now.
I am fifteen syllables shorter than a haiku.

Like you I have never been
to Durham or Barnard Castle
never been a member of any shadow cabinet.
I know nothing of Hank Marvin or Bruce Welch.
I play percussion
I play air guitar
but only to music that you like.
I have been blind all through your life
now like you I have only one eye
and my hair
which is as tangled as your syntax
is a little bit longer
now that you've let yours fall
over the head of the reindeer
on your Christmas jumper
which you wear all through the year
as if you were the shadow of Santa Claus.

If a Vaccine Can't Be Found

Some people are generous
some people give everything
the doctors and the nurses
and the care home workers.
The wolf and the recession
are on the horizon
the country is in the red
though not yet on the rocks
a light is flickering in the tunnel
idealism and social change
starts with a hand on the switch
wouldn't that be as lovely as Eliza Doolittle
with a bar of chocolate and a place to sleep.

The rich can take the hit
sell off a house in the country
a couple of ivory towers
a greenhouse in Greenwich.
Members of the public
members of Parliament
give a knife, a fork and a silver spoon
The rich and the poor coming together
the captain walking around the cabbages again
around the television screens of the island
around the world in a hundred years.
Let's get together to stop poverty
hunger and homelessness
spreading like coronavirus
give Eliza somewhere to live
away from the cardboard
and the cold night air
and not only that
give a pay rise to nurses.

I take off my red bandana
to the scientists searching for a vaccine
to Florence Nightingale
to Nye Bevan
to the doctors and the nurses
to the captain
to the journalists on the Guardian
and the *Plymouth Herald*
to the rich and the poor
who give both time and money.
I take off my sombrero
to the World Health Organisation
to the rockers and the rollers
to the ambulance drivers
to the beat poets
to the bobbies who may or may not be
your aunties and uncles
to the train drivers, the bus drivers
and Post-Modern Pat
to the merchants of the wind
the dispensers of food and medicine.
I rest my knife and fork
and charity shop spoon
I rest my briefcase
my reindeer jumper.
Sixty-seven million people
living on this island
from Lands End to John O'Groats
we're either all in this together or we're not
and not only that, George
if a vaccine can't be found by Christmas
will Santa Claus be furloughed.

Meeting Miss World

The flag is laying on the ground.
I've just hit my first shot
into the bluebells
narrowly missing
a group of conspiracy theorists
hanging out around the bunker.
They write messages to each other
with five irons in the sand
but only on cloudy days
because of satellites.
They see bugs in every ball
every wayward shot is a drone
a clandestine eye.
I don't know about you
but my secrets are about as interesting
as a shopping list in the pocket
of a crazy goalkeeper.
When they're not playing golf
they're waiting for the Apocalypse
but waiting for the Apocalypse
is like waiting for Miss World
to ask you out on a date.

A fortnight ago I hit an albatross
last week I hit another albatross
yesterday I got a letter
from Samuel Taylor Coleridge.

When I turned eighteen
in Nineteen Sixty-Nine
I had a dream of wearing
the green jacket like Orville Moody
by Nineteen Seventy-Two
I was living in a caravan and smoking weed

when I met you in Seventy-Three
I was hop picking outside Hereford
you opened the door to my caravan
and climbed inside my heart
took me grape-picking in Pauillac.
Looking back now to the clubhouse
of the late sixties
the television in my mother's house
is the closest I got to Carnegie.

Blind Mouse

I almost collide with a cyclist
while out walking in the city
through an avenue of trees
the cyclist mutters something
about parking meters
I apologise but point out
I'm pretty much blind
and in the middle of tripping
on three words that are so long
it'll take me eight hours
to pronounce them.
He looks at me strangely
turns from being a cyclist
into a psychedelic penguin.
I ask the cyclist why he doesn't have
a bell on the handlebars of his bicycle
he tells me he doesn't have a bicycle
in a voice as tight as bicycle clips.

As the fog lifts like rain on a reefer jacket
I notice that something soft and furry
is sniffing at my shoes.
When I look into the cyclist's face
I see that he's wearing dark glasses.
As he cycles off into the sunset
along Hoffman Drive
I lean against the trunk of a tree
run my fingers up and down the bark
as if reading braille
on a desk made of silver birch.
Now all I need is a flashback
of that time I saw an albatross
chatting to a rainbow
at a Dropping Huxley gig.

The Rook

On leaving home without a pen
the history of the day is lost
like a telephone number or a heart
closing my eyes has brought me here
to this place of strange faces
which one are you
Kafka, the film star,
the jackdaw or the waitress.
Everyone loves to play cards
at the cowboy movie table
to shuffle hearts and diamonds
to shoot derringers
to wear a sheriff's badge
over a Levi jacket
to be the quickest Art student
in the Wild West
to be the man who played guitar
with Ricky Valance
to play the man who got shot in Deadwood
to play the drums in Abilene
with the Grateful Dead.
The dead are carried out
through the bat-swing doors to the graveyard
where I first met the waitress
walking barefoot on Boot Hill
she makes me blush as she flaunts
her film star beauty
writes names and numbers into notebooks
with a black pen like a poet at a funeral.
When she walks out of shot
to make coffee in the kitchen
I sip wine with the old cheese crowd
stagger off home at the end of the night
to play jukebox jazz in the nursery rhyme dark

to read Kafka before falling asleep
in my semi-detached suburban castle.

On leaving home without paper and pen
I mourn the minutes
of meetings on street corners
that never get written down.
I move through this city
which is unknown to me
a city born out of the dust of night
a city of dream intoxicated fiction
which exists for a moment or for as long
as it takes the long finger of a train
to vanish into a pocket of fog.
As soon as I left home yesterday
the road back to it had gone
this is my country now where I stop
at a crossroads for a cup of coffee
stop for a year or two
or the rest of the night.
I take a key and a silver spoon
out of my pocket
spend a little tax haven cash
take the stairs to a rooftop room
plonk my shoulder bag down
go sleepwalking above the garage bands
and the car horns playing traffic jazz.
The next morning shortly after
the rooster let's rip
a door scrapes back the darkness of a room
veiled against the well lit streets
that brought me here.
I climb out of my sleeping bag
that unzipped heap of dreams
drop down into an armchair
to update my diary
to write a goodbye note to yesterday

to write a letter to my hometown's
three hundred thousand doormats.
As the ink dries over silver birch skin
I cross the room over a creak of footsteps
sleepily draw back the curtains to discover
the fading splendour of the Milky Way
in a telescope on the windowsill.
It must be the winter solstice.
If it isn't, it is now.

On leaving home on Christmas Eve
I go shopping for cards
to send to my grandchildren
living on the island of fish and chips.
Much to my surprise the film star
is working in the Post Office.
She drops my hidden kisses
into a bag over her shoulder.
I don't know her name
or how to bring her closer
but in the sequel shot the next night
she's dining out at the coven
of the oddly shaped table
in this city which has forgotten
to tell you its name
a city which is as old as birdsong
as old as the laughter on her bright red lips.
I take coins out of my pocket
for a hurricane on the rocks
take the last chair at the table.
Flicking through the pages of a young newspaper
I read the horoscope, starting with Aries
much to my delight the film star is sitting
next to the jackdaw
whose command of English is straight
out of the school of Richard Adams.
Hiding my smile

like a double vodka diplomat
I gaze out over the zodiac
of earth, air, fire and water
see that the jackdaw
is playing chess with Kafka.
Kafka's fingers are caressing the queen
the jackdaw's feathers are stroking a rook.
The film star makes her move
sweeping me away from star sign gazing
I look into her eyes
see that my undercover is broken
but not yet my heart
look down at her hand
to see if she's wearing a wedding ring
to see if her heart is covered with diamonds
but can't make out the shape of anything
resembling a husband underneath her gloves
and in that moment when our heads tilt
under some constellation of mistletoe
the waitress approaches the table
whispers something in Kafka's ear
as the moon moves over the cusp
the sun does its abracadabra thing
in the night sky.
The rain starts to fall
the rain makes a nice cup of coffee
the dream ends in mid-conversation
as we slip back through the curtains
that brought us here.
Punching in a combination of numbers
to another world
we drive there in an Alfa Romeo.

The Poetry of Leonard Cohen

It was the winter solstice
the last time we met
a year after the funeral
of an old friend
a year after I first began
to hear or sense
a whisper of change
it was the anniversary
or close enough
to that day of peace
that day of rest
that day of flowers
it was Monday afternoon.
Tuesday afternoon
Wednesday morning.
I was walking through town
a stranger in the time of coronavirus
I was passing through
the crossroads of the crowd.
down on Fortnight Square
when you stepped out of the supermarket
carrying a big rucksack of shopping.
After greeting but not shaking hands
I gazed over the rim of a red bandana
as you gazed over the rim of a blue bandana
and started talking about things on television
a world that's as distant to me
as two gunslingers on a spaghetti aisle.

The conversation drifted like clouds
like summer moving into autumn
like a busker changing key
you moved the conversation
to the poetry of Leonard Cohen

the nonsense verse of Edward Lear
you'd never spoken
to me about poetry before
so it was kind of strange
you were always ranting and raving
about the evils of global capitalism
but now the soap box had gone
though I could still sense
distant ghostly faces in the crowd
footsteps dancing closer
then stepping back in uncertain solidarity –
a congregation slowly converting to dust.

After a short break to clear
that nervous tickle in the throat
that void to fill with talk
I gazed at the Sunday morning crowd
moving up and down the street.
As the traffic lights behind your eyes
changed from red down to amber
down to goodbye, down to green
I sensed a disconnection
as if we were travellers
lost to each other
calling through radio fog
felt it even more so
when you asked about
the welfare of my wife
I've never been married
but sensing
that disconnection again
I told you she was fine.

On the way back home
I ran back through our conversation
the stuff on television
you planned to watch that night

the poetry and nonsense verse
of Leonard Cohen and Edward Lear.
I thought about marriage
thought about honeymoons
thought that maybe it wasn't you
but maybe it was me
that had forgotten
that snow white Saturday
behind the Blue Monkey
or that red hot fortnight on Hydra
the many-headed island
or sleeping side by side
in the city that never does
after going to the movies
to see Hermione Gingold
wearing a red bandana
Maurice Chevalier wearing blue
forgotten old anniversaries
of diamond and silver
or walking together
through Greenwich Village
reading the names of folk clubs
the names of rock bands
reading Rolling Stone
and the New York Times
reading the poetry of Leonard Cohen
the number plates of limousines
parked outside the Chelsea Hotel
in Nineteen Sixty-Four
Nineteen Sixty-Five
Nineteen Sixty-Seven.

Knives, Forks and Coffee Spoons

I live in an ivory tower.
How many silver spoons
it took to make this
I do not know.

I live with the grand-daughter
of a gambler who won it
in a game of cards
back in those bat-swing door days.
Bluffing the deck in Tombstone.

I live with the most beautiful of ravens
her hair is long and lined with silver.

I live in an ivory tower.
I make-believe it's not there.
If I could turn it into a tax haven
it would give the money
underneath your mattress
a place to sleep.
If I could turn it into a spaceship
I would travel to where
only Leonard has gone before
to somewhere that doesn't resemble here;
where the filthy rich play penny whistles
where the dirt poor play silver spoons
under wind stirred skies
the colour of milky coffee.

I live in an ivory tower
how many elephants
it took to make this
I do not know.

Waiting for News

I don't know when I'll see you again
but it won't be tomorrow afternoon
unless you're waiting in Bretonside
when I step off the bus
I may be wearing a visor or a red bandana
I may be slowly going off my rocker
or wearing colours that match
the shadows passing by in the dark.

There are strangers in my life now
strangers travelling undercover all over town
so many of them want the dance floor back
the weekends and the wild nights
but here at the end of October
it's as quiet as Christmas
I like the peace and the quiet
the point where the big city
becomes a small town
it reminds me of Chernobyl
after everyone left.

The telephone has taken
a vow of silence
the clocks went back last night
but an hour just isn't far enough.
Now and then I think about
moving out of this ghost town
now I write in the dark
to old friends reclining in exile
spend Halloween all by myself
while waiting for news from Oxford.

Discovering Little America

When Columbus discovered
what was already there
the Vikings had been and gone
the tribes were scattered
between Oregon and Texas
the big cities were mirages
out on the Mojave Desert.

When I was discovered
with a notebook and pen
in a drunken stupor in Little America
I was one of millions of people
living on this small island
out in the Atlantic
a long time after someone
from somewhere else
stepped ashore but kept it quiet.

When we discover rain
on some other planet
or learn how to travel
at the speed of light
will those discoveries
make all eight billion of us
feel a little less lonely
as we lift collective umbrellas
towards a dark mass
of beautiful black storm clouds
as another day passes
beneath the mouth-watering sky.

A piece of unidentified driftwood
may be discovered one day
touching the harbour wall at sundown

while the moon shines
like it did in childhood
like it will tomorrow night
shining down on the graveyards
of generations
on bonfires built by children
wearing yellow gloves against the cold
shining down on children playing leapfrog
playing science-fiction explorers in the park
playing the cow jumped over the rain puddle.

Getting Dressed in the Dark

You get dressed in the dark
take a hat off the dining room table
a black raincoat off the kitchen door
a reindeer jumper out of the wardrobe
to remind yourself and the world
that a reindeer jumper
just isn't for Christmas.

You take a bus conductor's shirt
off the back of your dad's old armchair
while humming a medley
of Stravinsky and Chopin
you add one piece
of clothing after another
until you look like a rainbow.

You cover your face with a red bandana
which you wore to a Wild West night
down on Michigan Gardens.
Slipping into shoes and odd socks
you call the film star
living on State Hill to tell her
that you don't know how much longer
this Jesse James audition is going to last.

Sixty-Nine

Sixty-nine
your hair not quite as long
at this end of the sixties
you run your fingers through it
as you walk across the room
recalling those days of love and peace
peace signs and flower power
back when a lysergic honeymoon
in San Francisco seemed so attractive
but after all these springs and summers
gone like rivers into the sea
you're still living here on this island
living in this city so many have left
but you still have the tears and the rain
the greenhouse and the grass growing
on the other side of the Honicknowle Hills
the long silver hair and the Dansette.

You look through the window
waiting for that point of invisibility
when everything darkens.
In the distance you see faces in the crowd
with the complexions of potatoes
the skyscrapers getting taller and taller –
Beckley Point, with a little help from Hoffman
turns into a birthday cake
burning hundreds of candles.
You walk back across the room
following something in your memory
an intersection that leads back to the past
back to hanging around with a shoulder bag
of words outside Pete Russell's
Hot Record Store on Market Avenue.

You see the sun going down
as you lower your eyelashes
a few minutes west of sleep.
You feel like running as if the sun
were a bus you just have to catch
the last bus that takes you home
to a house glowing with candles
eighteen teenage candles flickering
eight and a bit weeks to go
before leaving the sixties for the first time.

Sixty-nine
you open a box of swans
take a deep breath
long enough to last
a shooting star, a split-second.
As you let it go
the candle flames move
away from your lips.
Night falls as you gaze
across the bay at French windows
showing pinpricks of light.
You look up at the sky
see no-one walking on the moon
like you did that star twinkling night
running with old friends
in and out of the Atlantic;
playing American leapfrog
down at Devils Point
sixty-nine or thereabouts
as the years are numbered.

Take the Hand of Nancy Astor

I don't know what it is
that dropped into my dreams
undercover or under the influence
of overnight rain
but everywhere I look
I see the face
of the invisible man
the face with more twins
than a litter of Siamese cats
the face behind a crowd of masks
the mirage behind the curtain
peering into the sanctuary of the room.

When I leave the house
I see less and less people
out on the street
less and less people
with church bells in their eyes.
Is that you reading Jules Verne
in the City Centre
playing abracadabra
behind that gust of wind.

I like it when you read poetry
to a group of discernibly invisible friends
either on stage or on the doorstep
of impending winter.
When I clap with one hand in Japanese
and the other hand in English
I see the applause of ghostly molecules
a hand waving a greeting
in the cold north wind
a hand in need of a glove
a heart in need of electricity.

Is that you holding a spooky wand
in that land of mystical appliances

The ring around your finger has gone
like last night's marriage
like last night's dream
into some other bed.
The statue of Nancy Astor has vanished
after a night of fog on Elliott Terrace.
This is what happens
when the invisible man takes your hand.
Here dogs chase tennis balls across the grass
autumn dances a seasonal jig with winter
to the soundtrack of a song
written in Paris so long ago
a song of loss
a song of rain falling
out of a November sky.
Is that the invisible man's wife
or a catwalk model
dressed in a cloak of leaves
green fading to brown
under the sleepy trees
of old spring and summer
leaves making their getaways
from the homes of birds
who live by the sea
like children going out to play
they skip across the city.

At dusk I head out
into the traffic jam
eyes the colour of loss
peer out from the darkness
of Ghost Town Street
leaves fall on old suntans
friends become strangers.

It's hard but like the leaves
I've decided to let things go
until spring comes back with flowers.
I check the horizon
for ships and other things
but like the invisible man
and the leaves
so much has vanished from my gaze.
I sit here in this place where love
and language comes and goes
sit here and write these words
before forgetfulness takes them back.

Slowly Going Crazy

Six days of wallpaper is enough for me
another night of this and I'll go running
and screaming down the hill
to the Tumbleweed Hotel
calling your name
while slowly going crazy
out in the ghost town jungle.

Out on the road I count the cars
think about driving over to Prince Rock
to join a garage band
to boogie-woogie in a derelict nightclub
where the wind practices social whistling
where a psychedelic smile
hasn't been seen for weeks
where if it wasn't for the blue sky
it could be midnight.

On the cusp of sundown
I hitch a red bandana over my face
walk into the supermarket
check my lottery numbers at the kiosk
which comes up seven
short of the jackpot again
the dreams of another
Saturday-night millionaire
gone like cigarette smoke on the wind
which takes my hat as I cross the car park
throwing it like a tennis ball for me to chase.

The Other Side of the Rain Puddle

Down here on Ghost Town Street
I wear a mask in public
like that astronaut
like that train robber
like that politician
who was wearing a mask
long before he was wearing a mask.
I walk across town
in my cowboy boots
to the Wild West Park Building Society
open the door, open an account
in the name of Wild George Dollar.

On the last day
of the last month
the sun sets in the westcountry.
I kiss the old year goodbye
as I stand under the mistletoe
for a socially distant snog.

Night after night
I wipe the tears
of another weepy movie
off the television screen
think about getting a job
as a window cleaner
moving over to Hollywood
working in Beverly Hills.

Here on the other side
of the rain puddle
I have long conversations
with myself and others

muffled conversations
through the talking glass.

Here in suburbia
I go on another
fifteen minute fling with fame
gaze into the square eyes
of a sex symbol
make unattainable love on the sofa
go on a blind date to Specsavers
go on honeymoon to Blackpool.

Dropping Down in the West

I like to go out walking
through the city at night
down these badly lit streets.
This city – my hometown
resting on muddy hills
that shelters me in sleep and dream
this city where my gaze climbs
a man made mountain of windows
to stand a little closer to the moon
this city where I linger
like the last drop
of daylight in the west.

When night falls
I like to go out walking
with the younger
ghosts of myself.
Sixty-nine pairs of shoes
walking towards winter
in the rain and the wind.
Out here in the darkness
I have great fun
trying to tell the difference
between shadows and flesh
I walk into people
that aren't there
apologising as I fall
over nothing in the dark.

Belper

The cows come out at night
leave fields and farms
all over the country.
They drift through gates
down country lanes
a cattle drive
worthy of the wild west
but this is not Texas.

They make their way
through traffic jams in Dover
through fog in Barnard Castle
their calls can be heard
over the radio in Ambridge.
They mosey on down from Cowdenbeath
they pass through Chalk Farm –
after meeting the Minister of Agriculture
on Parliament Hill.
They slip over the Welsh border.

Down here in the westcountry
I hear them calling in Sherwell Park –
these makers of milk,
butter, cheese and yogurt.
They pass through Bullpoint
they kick up dust on Ernesettle Green
they moo mournfully on the banks
of Camels Head Creek
they stop for lunch in Freedom Fields.

Looking back down the years
I see children playing leapfrog
on a dozen village greens
as they jump over rusted spaceships

in a children's story
where stars are buttercups
where longhorns are movie stars
where a wolf howls at the moon
and the moon moos back
taking a giant step for herbivores
taking a giant leap for Belper.

The Last Year

It's the last day of the year
the last day of a long year
it's seven minutes to midnight
seven minutes
before a volcano of voices
lifts the town off its hinges
seven minutes
before the old year falls
in an avalanche of numbers
three hundred and sixty-five
of them cluttering the floor.
At seven seconds to midnight
a rocket breaks the silence
takes the old year out
on a last split-second waltz
around the dancehall.

Down here under the streetlights
where living through this last year
has seemed at times to be
a little bit like that sense
of anticipation you get
while sitting inside a waiting room
waiting for that lovely lonesome sound
of steam coming down the tracks.

Trapped between the past and the future
taking social distance to the extreme
I move millions of metres back to a time
when playing dominoes in a darkened room
doesn't make the headlines
back to a time when men
walked through sunlight on the moon
a time when I ran with other children

arms outstretched
flying in plimsolls across the grass.

Travelling back there now
Kick-starting the Velocette
slipping an old motorbike helmet
over long silver hair
I head for the blue-eyed past
leaving the last year to fall
like autumn into last night's sun
leaving twenty twenty
face outlawed against the wind
a stick-up man in a red bandana
a sixty-nine-year-old getaway driver
travelling in a convoy of mods and rockers
back to a childhood as familiar as dust.

Playing the Blues on Apsley Road

The girl on roller skates
wants to know
what happened to my eye
curiosity mixed here with innocence
in her words and gaze.
I could tell her
of the science of blindness
of which I know little
tell her that my eye is dreaming
that the left side
of my body is sleepwalking.

I take a medical file
out of my shoulder bag
thick as a dozen notebooks
blow dust off the jacket
which takes me back to that moment
skin dropped over light.
I tell the girl on roller skates
about the last forty years
placing my chin on the altar
of the split-lamp
down by the railway tracks
on Apsley Road
tell her about my days
out on the island
my years dressed as a pirate
swashbuckling finance with a white stick.

I look out over the sea
look at the moon moving it closer
tell her about the family of mermaids
I met on a fishing trip
while hitch-hiking out in the desert
mention the mirages that come and go

the science-fiction books I'd like to read
that were written on other planets.
tell her how I wanted
to be a landscape painter
and not sleep upside down
in a house made out of braille
writing poetry in a log book
ten degrees west of Caroline

Here in the midwinter darkness
I hear the soundtrack of the wind
the script of distant voices
calling through the fog.
As I look back through the years
I tell the girl on roller skates
how I was once runner-up
to Robert Louis Stevenson
in the World Swashbuckling Championship
tell her how I became a Box Office star
playing the part
of a buccaneer on Broadway
got nominated for nothing
not even an eye patch.

Taking a telescope out of my shoulder bag
I tell her how telescopes bring desert islands
bring super-novas closer
tell her I have a habit of reading poetry
over the phone to old friends
which is probably why they don't call
I tell her this
this story taller than a pirate on stilts
start to say goodbye
then as an afterthought
begin to recite my historic
circumnavigation of the Mewstone
not knowing that she's gone
roller skating into the sunset.

Gone to Make Coffee

It is gone midnight
the wind howls against the window
as you lean out into space
it whistles like a crazy dog caller
it takes your voice
takes language
throws it back
every note of birdsong
echoes made of sleep talk
mumbled conversations
under the radar of breath
a wild cacophony
conducted by a silver birch
a thin precious skeleton
stripped of its leaves
down at the end
of Grand Hotel Road.

It is gone Valentine's Day now
gone midwinter
gone gone gone
your brown eyes courting spring
the year is six weeks old
the night is as warm
as an old shilling
in the cupboard underneath the stairs
you book a bird's nest for the night
in a tree growing in the backyard
which throws itself around in a frenzy
like an oil painting in a landscape dance
the year has gone by like a newsflash
you have gone to throw teapots
into the Stonehouse mud
gone to make coffee.

It is April now
the clocks have gone
leapfrogging over Big Ben
into the future
half gone you look back
over your shoulder
to the Roundhouse on Chalk Farm Road
where you see a man
playing an air guitar
which looks like a Fender Stratocaster
to your invisible eye
his hair is long
but not yet silver
it is gone midsummer now
you write the longest poem of the year
read it over and over again to yourself
like a groundhog.

It is gone Halloween
gone Christmas Eve
gone midnight
gone Margaret Mitchell
gone Richard Burton
gone with the rockets
gone gone gone
or will be when you read this
down the telephone line
to the nightingale
who comes to your letterbox
with four sheets of paper
and a box of pens.

Shopping on the Table

I'm not much of a traveller
but if I were
I'd much rather trek
through the rain forest
than go shopping on the table.
When I look through
the empty window on the computer
I see nothing that makes me
want to go shopping with a mouse.

I go to work every day
even though the shops are closed.
I miss selling bits and bobs
miss the sound of the bell
tinkling above the door
the bread and butter pockets
of friends and strangers
now with all that gone
I hang out here most days
between nine and five
sing a little bit of Nashville
a little bit
of crosscountry and western.
I read Ghost Town Street's
evolving manuscript
to the mannequins
which makes me feel less lonely.
Every night when the street goes quiet
I take them out
window shopping around the mouse.

Pinball Lane

The land wears a white mask
mist clings to the face of the town
a fog horn blows out over the rocks.
Here on the edge of the sea
a shooting star falls
for those who sleep
in the arms of mermaids.
The much younger face of the moon
shines down on the body of a Viking
shines down on a slowly moving island
of Scandinavian wood.
Does the moon dream
of longships crossing space
of astronauts jumping up and down
like children on a bed.

The fog covers everything.
The compass beneath my shoes
guides me closer to home
where the future is filled
with correspondence from Friary House.
Sounds of the more recent past
fills the air with the joy of the familiar
as I make my way towards an allotment
on the other side of town
where a scarecrow is talking crazy to itself
telling fairytales to the wheelbarrow
to the cannabis plants
the sunflowers. the foxgloves.
As I get closer I can smell smoke
can hear an electric guitar
can hear the Groundhogs
on a radio in the greenhouse.
I can hear them through the glass

which is no more blue or yellow
than it is red or green.
If I could see through the mist
I might see the invisible man and his wife
dancing side by side on the floor
of this see-through nightclub
or stopping for a breather
when Tony McPhee's guitar slides off air
making way for Brian Protheroe's voice
which reaches me a minute or two later
forty-five revs away
at the other end of Pinball Lane.

Somewhere off in the mist
out on the streets
of this deserted town
a man in a mask
looks through the window
of a shop selling houses
while all over town
a mouse with a voluptuous appetite
nibbles away at the crowd.

The Millionaire

1

A shooting star
heading for the auction rooms
of London or New York
drops out of the unknown
passes through long grass
comes to rest, disintegrating
into a galactic jigsaw puzzle
on an island of cow dung.

Twenty thousand feet above the skyscraper
where the hitch-hiker lives
a love letter to Neptune, encased in glass
falls from a rocket passing over Firestone Bay
leaving an outer space ripple
out on the Atlantic.

A man with a metal detector
pops out of a Beverly Hills wardrobe
with a coat hanger and an aura of stardust.
A Miss World contestant
from the Twentieth Century
makes a living rummaging around
jumble sales and second-hand shops.
Yesterday she stumbled over
a Honeymoon Postcard bootleg
down at the Red Cross.
She goes out in the moonlight
a dozen weekends a year
comes back with bits and pieces
of the universe in her sack.
Here we have a piece of the Big Bang
here a chunk of a supernova
bidding starts at a hundred
and eighty-six thousand dollars

going under the hammer
going once
going twice
going to the millionaire
with the green suntan.

   2

The box of pens that wrote
the bulk of Ghost Town Street
if that box of pens sold at Sotheby's
they wouldn't fetch very much
not as much as my grandfather's
old rag and bone cart
his collection of horseshoes
or the pool of water
from some long forgotten snowman
found by archaeologists
under the floorboards at Stonehenge.
The supernova my mum and dad
kept in the shed
to keep the house warm in winter
is still shining like a shilling in the dark
while the longship discovered in the mud
down at Camels Head Creek
continues to keep
the fireplace bright with kindling.
If I could find the meteorite
that travelled thousands of years
to knock out Indiana Jones
I could save the box of pens
save the old rag and bone cart
save it for a rainy day at Christie's
along with the chess set
I nearly sold to that bloke
in the pawn shop on the Viaduct
that once belonged to Maurice Chevalier.

Six Days after the Jab

The wind blows kisses
from my house to yours
the rain seems to fall
with more vigour
six days after the jab
six days closer to the crowd
six days after I took
a call from Friary House
to roll-up my sleeve
to make it thirteen million.

I don't remember now
which year it was
when I came here last
to see a band that once played
with The Mothers of Invention
in Europe
but the closer I got
to the stage that night
the more the bass guitar
vibrated in my chest
all around me headbangers
were turning into amplifiers
then you dragged me back
you were my fire lady in blue jeans
you were my roadie.

Back here for the first time
in over twenty years.
The news from Oxford has arrived.
As I lift my Christmas jumper
back over my shoulder
I ask the nurse from Friary House
if I can have one for the reindeer

It's getting closer to Valentine's Day
but this is better than chocolate.
The last time I came here
Deep Purple
were playing at the Pavilions.
I only came to see them
with you that night
because I thought
you might like to dance.

Over the Rim of a Blue Bandana

The autograph hunter
meets the invisible man
and his bodyguard
meets the million dollar film star
meets the getaway driver
in the middle of a crowd scene
somewhere in a city
in Europe or America
faces grin in the dark
greetings are passed
like a packet of Rizla
over a coffee house table.

A door opens
in a hotel room in Verona
a pair of silk stockings
are draped over
the back of a chair.

A weepy movie cries to itself
in the dark corner of a room
in the district of Columbia
on a leafy street in Georgetown.

In democratic dreamland
a champagne cork takes off
in the hands of an astronaut
shortly after flying
a rocket to the moon.

In the minutes of the meeting
the film star passes a pen
and her hand across the table
for the autograph hunter to sign.

The film star would like to be
a waitress in a spaghetti western
would like to live
in a big house
made out of romantic fiction.
The autograph hunter's name is known to her
through searching second-hand bookshops.

After the meeting the film star
loses her face and a million dollars
in a game of cards
but gambles on taking it back as night falls.

The closer she comes to sleep
the closer she comes
to closing her innocent eyes.
Sleep is broken
but she feels strangely mended.

As dawn comes and goes
she sees it passing into history.
Leaving Wild West Park
the film star takes the bus into town
where she meets the autograph hunter
meets the invisible man and his bodyguard
in a multi-million dollar art gallery.
After asking for the bodyguard's autograph
the film star asks the autograph hunter
 to draw a portrait
of a married woman
on the palm of her wedding hand
and then to draw the portrait
of a bridesmaid
on the palm of her unmarried hand
and after that to draw a smile
on both of their faces.
When the paint dries

the film star slips on a pair of blue gloves
glances through the window at the unpainted city
then opens the door of the gallery
to let in a passing breath of summer air
she pauses and let's her gaze linger
for a confetti of seconds
on the landscape of an art school dropout.
As she hits the road
she lays a hand
on the shoulder of a passing shadow.

Moving out into the city
the film star walks back
through the ages of architecture
the bomb sites of sudden archaeology.
Slipping a cowgirl hat
over long silver hair
the film star thinks of herself
as the reincarnation of Bonnie Parker
or the not necessarily genetic
grand-daughter of Belle Starr.

Newsflashes follow her around.

The film star
calls herself Veronica
calls the autograph hunter Bonnie
calls the getaway driver Isabelle
in the blood red movie
they've yet to make.
The film star has a day to day face
which she wears day to day
the face she sees in the mirror
other faces bleed out of her dreams
faces she wears to work
down at the launderette.

These faces are absent
when meeting friends for coffee
meeting lovers for lunch
over at the Red Bandana
on Ghost Town Street.

Veronica never wears
her coffee drinking face
down to the launderette
where she works part-time
cleaning dirty pocket money
face masks and dresses.

Down in the cotton tunnels of the launderette
Veronica takes the painted faces of strangers
she met night-clubbing in her dreams
slips them into a shoulder bag
takes them out for a spin
window shopping
down on Daydream Boulevard.

You won't find Veronica's face
on any wanted poster
you won't find any undercover cops
down at the launderette
Veronica never leaves any fingerprints
she's a professional
and professionals always wear gloves.

When Veronica's not working
she goes down to the Post Office
sends romantic fiction manuscripts
to a post office box on the moon
to pen friends
living all over the planet.

Veronica wears her silver hair loose
sometimes she wears
Belle Starr's bandana
which fell off the back
of a stagecoach in Arizona
according to the guy
selling knives, forks and silver spoons
down at the car-boot sale.

Last weekend at the Dalton Bank
on Sundown Square
someone who didn't
look like Veronica
made last night's news
someone wearing purple hair
someone humming a guitar riff
that sounded like a cover
of Jimi Hendrix.
Even through the eyes of technology
Veronica couldn't make out
any signs of silver beneath the purple
or much of anything else through the haze.

Veronica smokes
home-grown cigarettes
a hundred and eighty-six
thousand watts of sunshine
glowing through her skin
as she drives
through ghost town streets
of red, green and amber
at sundown in a Bombed Out Beckley.
She'd like to move over
the rain puddle into the sunset
she's got a crush on outlaws
on drifters, on Clint Eastwood
but wonders why he's never

made a movie
down in the badlands
out on the hard shoulder
of Spaghetti Junction.

Over the last year
this silver-haired gunslinger
has worn a blue bandana
over bright red lipstick.
Like the autograph hunter
and the getaway driver
like the invisible man
and his bodyguard
she can't wait for things
to get back to some sort
of abnormal
but for now she has
last night's smile written
in bright colours on her face
and that's enough for now
enough for any outlaw abiding
devotee of moonlight
out window shopping in Coffeyville
on the long arm
of a sleeping policeman's shadow.

Down and Out on Downshire Hill

You take the train
from Hampstead to Chalk Farm
a trip of thirty-six or thirty-seven years
back to the past or into the future
one way or the other
the train is somewhere
on the tracks of the Northern Line.

You drop into the Roundhouse
on Chalk Farm Road
for a cup of coffee
the Roundhouse is crowded
with rock and rollers
and there's no sign of that dropout
from Wild West Park.
You drag a partly smoked three skinner
out of a bell-bottom pocket
think about that young dropout
with the same middle name as George.
You take a sip of coffee
slip out of your shoes
slip back to those days
to those garage band gigs
when you played rhythm and lead
with the Puppets of String Theory
back in those barefoot days
when you discovered Sandie Shaw.

Leaving the Roundhouse
at the end of the song
you walk back to the station
making tracks for Belsize Park.
Down in the underground
you hold a newspaper mask over your face

reading nothing as this tin bullet
rocks from side to side.
All the newspapers have different dates
they blur into one long commute.
Too much time travel
too much H.G. Wells
too much Doctor Who
too much innocence
too much acid or too much smoke.
It's all too fucking much.
You decide there and then
this isn't your planet.

Back home on Downshire Hill
you pay homage by lighting
candles to a ghost
you haven't got the breath
for blowing out all eighty-four
so you'll ask the wind
from West Hampstead
the wind from South End Green
for a little help
you'll call that young dropout
with the same middle name
as that ukulele player
you'll read him some Lorca
some Rosemary Tonks
maybe venture over to Parliament Hill
take in some crows
flying over that democracy
down by the river
a long way from Paris
a long way from Catalonia
you'll take his down and out hand.

The Radio Years

The radio isn't friendly
it doesn't play much music that I like
sometimes you'll get some Bruce Springsteen
sometimes some Joni Mitchell
but when do you ever hear
any Bob Dylan, Leonard Cohen
Desiderata Twang or the Gutter Biscuits
Suzanne Vega, J. J. Cale
Happy Baxter or Sonic Clutter.

If I had a show on a radio station
I'd call it the Radio Years
I'd play music you never
get to hear on the wireless
I'd play Calexico, James McMurtry
The Bottle Rockets, The Indigo Girls
Drive-By Truckers
and The Three Colours of the Road
and for an encore
and taking us up to the news
and back into pop land
The Bohemian Bootleg Orchestra
Zen in the Art
of Mobility Scooter Maintenance
Daydream Boulevard
and Twenty-Six Dollars
playing in velvet underneath the pillow.

Elm Road

I don't know if there are
any elm trees on Elm Road
as I've no idea
what an elm tree looks like.

I wouldn't be able
to tell the difference
between an elm leaf
or any other leaf
from any other tree
if it happened to fall

on my silver birch shoes
as I walked through
these ghost town streets
under the green
and brown of autumn
through Mannamead at midnight.

Rufus

After climbing the long
and winding stone staircase
eighty-seven steps that leads
from Compton's Priory Road
to Hartley's Hartley Avenue
you take a seat in the park
try to catch your late sixties breath
but your late sixties hands are too slow
your breath slips away
like a line of poetry
that never quite seems
to make the transition
from the mind to the page.
As you take a deep shot of air
from the lips of a hurricane
talking in its sleep
you ask yourself
and you ask the wind
how much of your breath is Katrina
how much of it is Imogen
but the wind isn't talkative
or the wind is secretive
or the wind doesn't know.

You take a landline out of your pocket
with the longest extension lead in the world
call the Katrina Line to ask
if they're going to call the next hurricane
after the girlfriend who blew you away
with her beautiful smile.
While waiting patiently
a hand at the other end
of the rainbow hangs up
a hand covered in red sellotape

a hand covered in raindrops.
Disappointed, you call the switchboard
down at the Tumbleweed Hotel
for a mythological alternative
an indigenous fairytale –
the name the wind gave itself
gave its invisible siblings.
A magpie calls out a suggestion
from the other side of the park
calls a name with too many syllables
a name longer than a freight train
a name which even
the invisible troubadours of Hartley
the chatter-boxing sparrows can't pronounce.
The name of the wind
is a lovely long jazz-like solo
playing in the park in the key of crow
a name augmented
by the feather bands of winter.
Yet again you ask the wind
how much of your breath
is the breath of Imogen
how much of the wind is Katrina
how much the name
a mother gives a child.

Blowing out a little smoke-scented breath
you begin to write a long letter
to the poetic heart of Compton
to the crows flying from tree
to tree like woodland inspectors
to the ghost of a dog called Rufus
barking peacefully in the quiet rooms
of the house at night.
In homage to Rufus
a tennis ball drops out of your sleeve
another drops into your hand

after dropping out of a bohemian pocket.
You throw them experimentally
until they vanish
like half-remembered dreams
gone with the dark
gone with the moon
running at tennis ball altitude
through the long grass.

It's peaceful sitting here with Rufus
the silence only broken every now and then
by the voices of strangers greeting each other
on the other side of the hedge.
Birds sing in the park
trees stir slowly out of winter's slumber
nothing moves in the air
not a butterfly breaking out of sleep
nothing big enough for the eye to catch
or Rufus to chase.
The sky is jam-packed with clouds
they only sing when it rains
white as primary school chalk
they drift over the distant rooftops
of Crownhill and Efford.

The sun moves in and out of cover
passes over Hartley Avenue
shines down over the stone staircase
that leads back to Priory Road.
The sun brings out
the dark shadows of your lifeline
as it moves across the page
you read the words you've written
but predict nothing
cross the palm of your hand
with a strand of silver hair
you call landlines

call Katrina and Imogen
call Rufus through the dog flap
in the kitchen wall.

A pair of sleep drifting nightingales
pass through this peaceful room of a day
are they friends of Rufus
moving in and out of the blue
or mirages in the sky.
You would drift off with them
but your wings are wishes
that wouldn't make it as far
as a tennis ball rolling across the grass
to meet Venus in Flushing Meadow
to meet Katrina in New Orleans.

Summer moves closer
sun rays run fingers
through long silver hair.
A shadow stretches out
under a log fire sky.
A family of scarecrows
remove hats and coats
creating a charity shop
installation on the grass.
The sun warms
the stone cold doorsteps
of Compton and Hartley
melts the polar ice caps on your fingers.
Sparrows insert musical chatter
into the soundtrack of the day.
As you wish you wish you could
read these words to them
in the key of a songbird
or sing like Rufus
barking in dog decibels
resting here in this garden
until spring comes out of the ground

wish a million wishes were enough
to inherit a key that opens a door
to a three bedroom house
a place to drop your name on a doormat
to write love poems in every room
to immortalise its architecture
to write as crows fly home over Henders Corner
to write love letters to the dogs of peace
to let Rufus run free to haunt
the leafy lanes and cul-de-sacs
to lay your head down when night comes
to fall asleep on the wild slopes of Compton.

The voices of dog walkers
bring you back down to seaside level
they slip over the hedge
slip over your shoulder
over the ghostly bark of Rufus
then the quiet returns as does the sun
yet still you linger
you don't want to leave
the magic of this place
but know you must.
You wave an orchestral wand
in a flourish to summon
a house out of the ground
then remind yourself you're not a tree
waiting for birds to migrate
back home to England
waiting for leaves to return
waiting to wear them like gloves
hundreds of green pairs
slipping over long brown fingers.
You're not waiting for a taxi
you're waiting like Rufus
for spring to move out of winter
as cherry blossom begins to fall
at such a young age.

Hartley Park

Away from the city
the quiet moves in
like a soft embrace.

Cars out on Mannamead Road
act as a reminder.

A magpie touches down
out of the unknown
a counterpoint
to a counterfeit world.

The cherry blossoms bloom
flamingo-leafed
on the springtime slopes.

The roundabouts and swings
are made out of childhood magic.

A dog comes with greetings
a feather drops out of the air
a postcard slips through a letterbox
on Hartley Park Gardens.

You look out over the houses
houses with eyes
much older than yours
with cracks that could be smiles.

You see a crow
coming down to feed
on the green
lunch table of the grass
like you it dines

with two or three friends
or it dines alone.

You can see that
what the world needs now
is more playgrounds
more roundabouts
more swings
more see-saws like the ones
sticking through that big long fence
on the border of Mexico and America.

Ursula

    1

What you need right now
is to take your shoes
away from the wallpaper
drop out into the noise
away from the voices in your head
away from socialising with house flies
Pick up your briefcase
your ink-stained notebook
chock-a-block with post modern dust
when you reach the corner
of Ghost Town Street
bypass as much midweek traffic as you can
lose yourself in the back lanes of Greenbank
then cut across to Freedom Fields
that old Victorian nightingale on the hill
try to imagine your blue-grey eyes
looking through a post-war window
its November
you've just missed Hallowe'en
there are leaves and rockets in the sky
its seven and a bit weeks to Christmas
but you don't know that yet.
Note the absence of storks
which some years later
slipped into the narrative of mythology
only to vanish again.
Note the long gone models of cars
names once so familiar
now lost to you as they slowly
drive up the hill from the direction
of Beaumont Park.
Turn your blue-grey eyes
west for a moment

over the rooftops to the train station
five minutes by pram
to the house where you lived as a child
around the corner from Wyndham Square
in the quiet years after the war.
Look into the future
sense the nostalgia
waiting patiently in the past
tuck those memories away for now
let other memories loose
drifting over the rooftops of Mutley Plain
now glimpsed in the distance
five minutes by walking stick
to Cheltenham Place.

2

Walking through the heart of the city
you dip your pen into the river
and there you dream of Ursula
there you dream movies
that never star Redford or Coburn
or anyone who crossed
your childhood gaze.
There are narratives here
slipping down side streets
tangents waiting on every corner
distractions to lure you
fairytales to enchant
memories hidden under
the closed eyes of bar rooms.
There are dropouts
smoking reefers on Lisson Grove
dropping out to write fiction
dropping out to write free verse
it comes out of stardust
comes out of a fistful

of twenty pound notes
the past lives here
in a room above your shoulders
it slips out of a briefcase
out of a pocket
a pen searching for a notebook
to lay words down
in an ink-free zone
before the voices in your head
slip back into silence, into solidarity.

Your gaze drifts across the road
to the Hyde Park Hotel
where nothing moves out on the island
where that collective silence
stretches into April.
You could live here
a freeloader writing free verse
dropping the Queen into the jukebox
playing the Rolling Stones
in a nod to irony.
On some future weekend
when the doors of the hotel
are flung open
it'll be like November
there'll be rockets all over town
like there were on that bonfire night
when you went to a Language Club reading
in a room above the bar
the night a rock band opened
for Lee Harwood and Helen Macdonald.

Moving closer to the island
lit up in red and amber
you walk with the green man
under the ever changing
colours of the road

looking up you see that
the hotel's brightly lit windows
have now grown dark.
As you cross the road
with your unvaccinated shadow
you see curtains move
sense the eyes of bartenders
looking out, marooned in lockdown.

Turning in the direction of North Hill
you travel back through the years
set somewhere between
ballroom dancing and punk rock
you see memories
popping out of the darkness
old friends hanging around
on street corners
flashbacks flickering into life
on the screen of the old Belgrave cinema.
As you begin to close the door
on these titbits of suburban fiction
you stumble on a memory
of desert island Dansette nights
smoking weed on Connaught Avenue
talking psychedelic rock with Roy Plomley
plonking you feet under Angie's table.
You see yourself crossing the doorsteps
of second-hand bookshops
in desert island boots or plimsolls
before heading back home
to the Tumbleweed Hotel to read
Marion Zimmer Bradley
Michael Moorcock
Larry McMurtry.

Leaving Mutley Plain
you take off on another shoestring tour

through the posh part of town.
After the leafiness of Wilderness Road
you reach the summit of Hill Crest.
Laying down your free verse flag
you discover there's more than one house
on Hermitage Road.
Here on the hill overlooking the city
you see the dark eyes of clouds
overlooking the ground.
As the rain starts to tumble out of the air
it falls from your eyes in solidarity.

3

In a hat trick nod to Charlie Chaplin,
Acker Bilk and John Cleese
you take a bowler hat
out of your briefcase
you recall carriages of bowlercrats
reading broadsheets
travelling home to Highgate
like some underground spy ring
on the Northern Line.
You try to recall a time
when bowler hats ever formed
or complemented
part of a pinstripe period
down here in the seaside sticks
but nothing pops out of the trilby.
If bowler hats had ever been worn here
then the chances are
they would have been worn
in the vicinity of Henders Corner
but in another lifetime
as the crow flies or the frisbee
but even that feels
slightly anachronistic

as does the notion
of crows playing frisbee
in or out of any pinstripe period.

Out on Mannamead Road
you try to remember the names
of other writers who've lived here
Adele Seymour
Francesca Henderson
Veronica Russell
Harriet Carrington-Fisher
George Braithwaite
Gabrielle Lane.
The straw hatted surrealists
of Mannamead and Hartley
who've always reminded you
of a posh spy ring in Portmeirion
Cambridge
Newton Ferrers
Noss Mayo.

Taking a seat in Thorn Park
you call a friend in Freedom Fields
to tell her that you've
decided against defecting
to the Red Bandana
on Ghost Town Street.
Ending the call you write a note
to the voices in your head
listing some of the things
you'd like for Christmas
a pair of grungy trousers
a clarinet
a slapstick movie
with the sound turned down.

Leaving Thorn Park
you turn your blue-grey eyes
towards spending some time
dancing with Ursula
to a little bit of trad jazz
a little pink elephant waltz
under trees taller than houses
where a leafy decadence
lingers in the air.

The Narrow Road to the Deep West

The park takes
its name from the trees
it arrives in March
it's gone by April
it travels all over the world
last year a tennis court
was discovered by explorers
in the Amazon Rain Forest.

The park leaves a park sized
photograph of itself
its current location is unknown
it could be in Wimbledon
could be on Hydra
in Newton Ferrers or Noss Mayo
could be out on the Mewstone
on the bottom of your shoes
or in a green convoy
out on the narrow road
to the deep west
passing over a moon gazer
reading Basho on the grass.

If you fancy spending
most of April
and all of May in Paris
June and July in New York
August and September in Montevideo
the rest of the year
out on the road
bring a lawnmower and a sleeping bag
over to the park
when the cherry blossom starts to fall.

The Long Lost Shadows of Saturday Night

I've travelled all over the world
from Noss Mayo to Newton Ferrers
for a while I wrote letters
which were never much longer
than a shadow crossing the street
on a Saturday night.

At seventeen I made
the acquaintance of weed
mushrooms and magic
At thirty-seven
I began writing a sequence
of poetry which I sent
cross country to an old lover
living at the haunted end
of Ghost Town Street.

A traveller from my teenage years.
A museum dedicated to my collected shoes
would be a step in the Kerouac direction.

Now at sixty-nine
I'm returning to my suburban roots.
Now I'm back, what I'd like to know
in a couple of tomorrows
is if my writing desk
is part cedar, part redwood,
part of the rain, the wind, the forest
whether any of the trees
would know in Central Park
either here or in New York.

The Ghost Writers Club

for Thom Boulton

Words linger on your lips
like the sweetness
of a Suzanne Vega song
every time you read to yourself
every ghost writer in the room listens.

A first draft of free verse
drops into the accumulated dust
of years on your writing table
your pen has done a bunk
into the domestic clutter
so you write and you write
your latest masterpiece
with a stick of chalk
like a primary school teacher.

The sun slips under the door
of your writing room
makes the house shine
your eyes follow it
until it slips into the west.

Darkness falls
like a power cut.
Sleep is a stranger
who comes in the night
doesn't tell you its name.

The darkness isn't afraid of itself
the darkness is afraid of the light
but has learned to push
the scary blueness away.

Unseen by you a ghost writer
looks nostalgically over your shoulder
as it takes a short cut
through the architecture
of the Ghost Town Street
Ghost Writers Club.

You take a break
from making language
out of a city
out of a white space
you take a flashback
of a nineteen sixty-seven
transatlantic telephone call
into the kitchen
which is interrupted
by a very noisy washing machine
reading ink stains to itself.

You think about leaving here
knowing it's not easy to leave
the road you've travelled
to go guitar solo all by yourself
to hear that lonesome sound
and not sigh
when a steam train leaves town
in a grumble of smoke.

Reading Baudelaire in April

for Melisande Fitzsimons

The invisible man
takes the spaceship
out for a science-fiction spin
to an unidentified park
on the eve of Baudelaire's
two hundredth birthday.
The invisible man's wife
stays at home
reading poetry in the kitchen
first she reads a collection in French
then she reads a collection in English
then she writes a letter
to the ghost of a novelist
living behind a pin-striped letterbox
then she lights two hundred candles.

The following night
the invisible man takes the rocket
over land and over sea
over the rooftops of Paris
parks it in a garage
on the banks of a river
climbs out
of a star-spangled spacesuit
makes a cup of coffee
drops in a lump of sugar
lights a little bit of home grown
with one of Baudelaire's candles
pops a couple of stargazers
opens a bottle of red wine
the night taking off like a rocket
a supernova of old news
flashing across the sky.

The invisible man's wife stays at home
writing poetry in the kitchen
first she writes one in French
then she writes one in English
filling the darkness with words
filling her mouth
with waterfalls of champagne
until the pen runs out of light
the candles run out of ink
the darkness blows out the sun.

Ghost Town Year

Back in those road-free days
set in a suburban childhood
where a dream of driving
one of the cars
you'd seen on television
through a string of towns
on the other side of the Atlantic
a hundred miles an hour
on a long road through America
driving out of Detroit
down to San Francisco
jamming with a rock band
at a love and peace weekend
in some back street garage
driving on the wrong side of the road
in a black Suburban Shuffle
a notebook with Amelia's name
and number on the dashboard
a guitar acquainted
with Blind Boy Kennedy's fingers
quietly strumming to itself
in a boot covered with rust
and ghost town stickers
a memory of Celestine
waving goodbye or goodnight
in a film shot on a supermarket aisle
in some border town you passed through
where you're cast as a stranger
gazing at footage
flickering in a small town window.
You look up at the sky
your face covered by a mask
looking back at the screen
you see the moon shining
off the coast of California or Texas.

Those road free days
made a comeback last year
when car drivers stayed at home
making strawberry jam
when dog walkers were spotted
throwing tennis balls on Greenhouse Road
the grass grew long and so did your hair.
Last year you gave the city
a bunch of new street names
last year in a place of cigarette smoke
a place of environmentally hazardous fog
driving a piece of twentieth century tin
through the quiet neighbourhood
around Fortnight Square
a traveller passing through town
stopped to gaze at a sequel of loneliness
flickering in a corner shop window.
Last year weekend after weekend
Saturday nights impersonated
Sunday mornings and there
in the suburban blues darkness
at the end of yet another long day
the broken hearted came out to weep
buckets and buckets
of twelve bars at midnight
came out to see the rain falling
over the sleeping streets
back in that ghost town year
when you walked in the unvaccinated dark
all by yourself through the shadows.

Looking for Yellow

for Dan Hartigan

I believe anything
I believe Dan Hartigan
when he says
there's no such colour as yellow.
I'm gullible like that
but I'm not sure
where that leaves custard
or the trousers that change colour
when I trip.

If I looked all night
would I find yellow
lurking in the lysergic darkness
under a flower power rug
in one of the rooms
of the Tumbleweed Hotel.

A word like yellow
when written down has something
of the chameleon in its genes
when it spills out of the pen
as blue or black ink
changing colour in translation.

If buttercups and dandelions
form part of a staple diet
of a yet to be discovered
vegetarian chameleon
then maybe yellow exists
but only after lunch or breakfast
down in the darkness
at the end of that long tongue.

If yellow has been wiped out
by the painters and decorators
who designed and gave second coats
to the sun and the moon
does this mean there are now
only six colours of the rainbow
unless I'm wrong about
the colour of bluebells
or the foxgloves that grow wild
in David Attenborough's greenhouse.

If sunflowers have changed colour
to wedding dress white
what colour is the invisible groom's hat
the invisible bride's dress.

If yellow is not yellow
what colour is the submarine
that sank beneath the waves
on pirate radio.

Waiting for William

for William Telford

Laughter from the kitchen
reminds you of comedy sketches
around dishwash at the weekend
your hair hidden under a hat
your left eye sleeping
a story which seems
to fascinate young children
like here on the corner
of Ghost Town Street
where you sit waiting for William
to walk through the door
and order Christmas cake
now that autumn's here
but he's late or has been delayed
by another newsflash.

Somewhere between Pentangle
and Patrick McGoohan
a siren cuts through afternoon traffic
as darkness falls across the sky.
Out on the street
someone calls to Santa
through a car window
soon be time
for hedgehogs to hibernate
soon be time for Christmas jumpers.

The moment you stop writing
your pen falls asleep in your hand
spilling ink all over your skin
for the gypsy to read.
If not tonight, maybe tomorrow
you'll dream of red wheelbarrows

dream of a chicken with white feathers
and all because of clouds
all because of daffodils
all because of blueberry muffins
you'll dream of reading with William
somewhere on Frankenstein Gate.

Gosport

After taking my postcode
the man on the booster line
asks me if I know
Brockhurst's Pharmacy in Gosport.
I tell him it's in Hampshire
he tells me it's the nearest
vaccination centre to where I live
I tell him that I live
hundreds of miles away
down on the Cornish border
here in Speedwell City
twenty minutes from my seaside home
to the banks of the Plym
the banks of the Tamar.

After giving him my postcode again
the man on the booster line
asks me if I know
the address of the football ground
I tell him it's in Central Park
he tells me that Central Park
is in New York
along with Manhattan and Brooklyn
I tell him
that I live in Bretonside
tell him I'll take a taxi
down to the Mayflower Steps
spend the weekend in Greenwich Village.

Goodbye Ghost Town Street

for Thom Boulton

Remember those Springtime days in Millbay Park
making contact with the 21st Century again
reading stuff written in Hibernation
back when hedgehogs lay sleeping
four to a bed
under the not yet sunny ground

Remember those Springtime days in Thorn Park
reading to each other
overlooking Thorn Park Lodge
which became our winter home
remember that spring and summer
dreaming of reading all over town
in Freedom Fields and Ghost Henge Park

Remember sitting in a grassy circle
looking down over the slope
at the swings and roundabouts
and the seesaws in Mutley Park
where we read to the trees
and the birds in the distance
the redwood and the goat willow
the crow and the albatross

Remember that old red bandana
that dropped to the ground on Ghost Town Street
the year before we inherited
the family trees sycamore and silver birch
the year the world gave back to us
the keys to the door

Glossary

Many locations in Plymouth and its environs are mentioned in the poems, and we thought they needed referencing for those who do not know the area. Likewise, cultural references that seem unexceptional to the author and the publisher probably do need some explanation for younger readers, the existence of Wikipedia notwithstanding.

LOCATIONS IN PLYMOUTH

Apsley Road — road that runs alongside the rail line in Mutley, and former site of the Royal Eye Infirmary..

Beaumont Park — green space off to the eastern end of the city centre.

Beckley Point — student accommodation near the rail station.

Blue Monkey — pub in the St Budeaux district of the city, and about 5 minutes' away from the author's childhood home. It burned down in 2006.

Bretonside — location of the old bus station.

Bullpoint — site of former military barracks, between the River Tamar and the St Budeaux district.

Camels Head — district just south of St Budeaux; also home to Shakey Bridge.

Camels Head Creek — tidal waterway flowing into Plymouth Sound

Central Park — large park in the centre of Plymouth, and site of the Plymouth Argyle football stadium.

Chatsworth Gardens — in Honicknowle; the author's childhood home.

Cheltenham Place — in Mutley.

Compton — suburb of Plymouth, located between Mannamead and Efford.

Crownhill — district immediately to the east of Honicknowle (q.v.).

Derriford — large district to the north of Plymouth and location of the region's biggest hospital.

Dorothy Ward Lane — in the Barbican.

Efford — eastern suburb of Plymouth, with post-war housing.

Ernesettle Green — open space in Ernesettle, west Plymouth, near the River Tamar.

Freedom Fields — hospital, where the author was born.

Friary House — GP surgery near Beaumont Park.

Greenbank — Victorian area of the city between Mutley and the centre; once the location of a major hospital.

Hartley / Hartley Avenue — suburb on a hill to the north of the centre.
Henders Corner — junction of Mannamead Road and Eggbuckland Rd.
Hermitage Road & Hill Crest — in Mannamead.
Honicknowle — district where the author grew up.
Lisson Grove — in Mutley.
Mannamead — leafy suburb north of the city.
Market Avenue — in the west of the city centre.
Mayflower Steps — steps and archway supposedly marking the point at which the "pilgrims" embarked on the Mayflower for North America. Plymouth, Mass., has a similar monument for their arrival point.
Mewstone — small rocky island off Wembury Point; access is restricted. Controlled by the National Trust.
Mutley Plain — shopping street north of the city centre.
North Hill — road connecting Mutley Plain with the centre.
Pavilions — concert arena.
Pete Russells — indie record store, much beloved by those of an alternative persuasion in the 1960s and '70s.
Plym — river that used to mark the eastern boundary of the city, and gives the city its name.
Prince Rock — area to the east of the centre, on the way to Laira Bridge.
Priory Road — in Compton.
Sherwell Park — alternative name for Drake's Place, a small park close to North Hill and across from Sherwell Arcade.
Tamar — river to the west of the city marking the border between Devon and Cornwall.
Thorn Park — in Mannamead.
Wilderness Road — in Mannamead.
Wollaton Grove — in Honicknowle.
Wyndham Square — in Stonehouse, to the west of the centre.

Locations near Plymouth
Newton Ferrers and Noss Mayo — twin coastal villages to the east of Plymouth.

People and Other Places
Richard Adams (1920–2016), British novelist, especially known for *Watership Down*.
Nancy Astor (1879–1964), American-born British MP for Plymouth Sutton, the first woman to sit in the British Parliament.
Acker Bilk (1929–2014), clarinettist, popular in the 1960s.

Ambridge — fictional location in BBC Radio 4's long-running drama *The Archers*.

Barnard Castle — in Durham; much in the news during the pandemic when a certain government adviser travelled there when he wasn't supposed to.

Basho (1644–1694), Japanese poet and writer, especially famous for his haiku, and *Narrow Road to the Deep North and Other Travel Sketches*.

Belper — town in the Amber Valley, Derbyshire.

Belsize Park — in Hampstead, London.

The Bottle Rockets — US rock band from Missouri, founded 1992.

Marion Zimmer Bradley (1930–1999), SF and fantasy novelist best-known for the Arthurian novel, *The Mists of Avalon*. Some awkward biographical details emerged after her death which have severely damaged her reputation.

J. J. Cale (1938–2013), US guitarist, from Tulsa, Oklahoma.

Calexico — US indie-rock band from Tucson, Arizona, founded in 1996, named after the eponymous city.

Paul Celan — German Jewish poet (1920–1970) born in Romania, who lived in Paris for most of his adult life and produced some of the greatest poetry in German in the 20th century.

Cowdenbeath — town in West Fife, Scotland, near Dunfermline and Edinburgh.

Dansette — British brand of portable record-players, popular in the 1960s.

Drive-By Truckers — US rock band from Athens, Georgia, founded 1996.

John Cleese, b. 1939. Star of *Monty Python* and *Fawlty Towers*, etc.

Downshire Hill — street in Hampstead, London.

Hermione Gingold (1897–1987), British actress with a long Hollywood career.

Lee Harwood (1939–2015), British poet. Shearsman Books published his *New Collected Poems* in 2023.

The Indigo Girls — US folk-rock duo, active since 1985.

Jack Kerouac (1922–1969), US beat writer, most famous for his novel *On the Road*.

Federico García Lorca (1898–1936), great Spanish poet and playwright, murdered by Franco's forces.

Helen Macdonald (b. 1970), British writer and naturalist. Originally a poet (*Shaler's Fish*, 2001), she later gained considerable fame as a result of her prize-winning book, *H is for Hawk*.

Patrick McGoohan (1928–2009), US actor, especially well-known for the TV series *Danger Man,* and the iconic *The Prisoner*.

James McMurtry (b. 1962), US musician, son of Larry.
Larry McMurtry (1936–2021), US writer, mainly of westerns.
Tony McPhee (1944–2023), British guitarist and leader of the rock band, The Groundhogs.
Orville Moody (1933–2008), US golfer. Winner of the US Open, 1969.
Michael Moorcock (b. 1939), British writer, best-known for his SF and Fantasy novels.
The Mothers of Invention — US rock band founded in 1964 by Frank Zappa, and largely a vehicle for his compositions.
Bonnie Parker (1910–1934), one half of "Bonnie and Clyde".
Pauillac — town in the Gironde, S.W. France.
Pentangle — British folk-rock band active from 1967. The original line-up was something of a super-group: Jacqui McShee (vocals); John Renbourn (vocals and guitar); Bert Jansch (vocals and guitar); Danny Thompson (double bass); and Terry Cox (drums).
Roy Plomley (1914–1985), British broadcaster and creator of the never-ending *Desert Island Discs* programme.
Portmeirion — folly tourist village in Wales, filming location for *The Prisoner*.
Brian Protheroe (b. 1944), British songwriter and actor; famous for his song, 'Pinball'.
Rizla — British brand of cigarette papers
Sandie Shaw (b. 1947), hugely successful British pop singer in the 1960s.
Sonic Clutter — one of the author's imaginary bands, or a covers band from Texas: which came first? Answers on a postcard to the chicken or the egg.
Specsavers — British high-street chain of opticians.
Speedwell — a ship that accompanied the Mayflower to America in 1620; however it turned back half-way and returned to Plymouth.
Belle Starr (1848–1889), US outlaw, associated with Jesse James.
Stonehouse — one of the original "three towns" of Plymouth. To the west of the centre.
Rosemary Tonks (1928–2014), British poet and novelist. She dropped out completely following her conversion to an extreme form of fundamentalist Christianity, and published nothing for the last five decades of her life. All of her poetry has been republished since her death as well as some of the novels.
Ricky Valance (1936–2020), Welsh pop singer, best remembered for 'Tell Laura I Love Her' (1960), a million-selling cover of a US hit record.
Suzanne Vega (b. 1959), US singer-songwriter.

www.ingramcontent.com/pod-product-compliance
Lightning Source LLC
Chambersburg PA
CBHW031635160426
43196CB00006B/431